LAMBROS

LAMBROS

DIONYSIOS SOLOMOS

Translated with introduction and notes
by
MANOS GEORGINIS

Shoestring Press

All rights reserved. No part of this work covered by the copyright hereon may be reproduced or used in any form by any means – graphic, electronic, or mechanical, including copying, recording, taping, or information storage and retrieval systems – without written permission of the publisher.

Typeset and printed by Q3 Print Project Management Ltd,
Loughborough, Leics
(01509) 213456

Published by Shoestring Press
19 Devonshire Avenue, Beeston, Nottingham, NG9 1BS
(0115) 925 1827
www.shoestringpress.co.uk

First published 2006
© Copyright: Manos Georginis
The moral right of the author has been asserted.
ISBN-13: 978 1 904886 27 3
ISBN-10: 1 904886 27 2

Shoestring Press gratefully acknowledges the financial assistance of the AG Leventis Foundation.

ACKNOWLEDGMENTS

Thanks are due to John Lucas, Professor Emeritus at the Universities of Loughborough, and Nottingham Trent for proof-reading the text and making valuable suggestions.

My thanks are also due to George Dandoulakis, Lecturer in English in the Dpt. of Humanities and Social Studies at the Hellenic Army Military Academy (Athens) for his help in proof-reading and preparing the typescripts.

I would also like to thank Rvd. George Metallenos, Professor of History at the School of Theology, University of Athens for providing me with his published work on Solomos and allowing me to quote extensively from it.

For Fotini

CONTENTS

Introduction	1
Solomos' Life	1
Solomos the Poet	3
Lambros	9
Notes on the Translation	17
Lambros (fragments) – Plot	21
Maria's Grudge	23
Maria's Dream	24
The Martyr	26
Lambros with his Daughter	27
Two Songs Sung by Maria	
The Two Siblings (song)	28
The Mad Mother or the Cemetery (Song)	34
The Confession	40
Easter Sunday	41
Maria's Prayer and Lambros' Vision	42
The Evening of Easter Sunday	42
Maria's Madness	45
The Death of Lambros and Maria	46
Various Fragments	48

INTRODUCTION

SOLOMOS' LIFE

Dionysios Solomos was born on the Ionian island of Zakynthos (Zante) in 1798, the illegitimate child of Conte Nicholas Solomos (Salamon in Italian) and his maid-servant, Angeliki Niklis, a fifteen-year old girl. The sixty-one year old count was married and had two other children. Since 1796 he had been living with Angeliki, who, besides Dionysios, gave him another son, Demetrios, in 1802.

The Salamons originally came from Crete, which was under Venetian rule. A year after the island fell into Turkish hands (1699), the Salamons journeyed to Zante as refugees. The Venetians in Zante acknowledged all the privileges that the Cretan refugees had enjoyed in Crete. Later, in 1699, the family was given the Venetian title of count.

One day before he died, the poet's father married the servant girl and both Dionysios and Demetrios were legitimated and received their fair share of the family estate. A few months after her husband's death, the poet's mother remarried.

When Dionysios turned ten, his legal guardians sent him to Italy with his tutor, the Italian abbot Santo Rossi. At home, he spoke demotic Greek with his mother, but his formal education was in Italian. Santo Rossi was a political refugee, who had fled to Zante from Cremona, and it was to that city that he took Dionysios. At high school Dionysios attended classes in Italian and Latin. His teachers were members of the Italian radical circles. In 1815 he left school and studied Law at the University of Pavia, from which he graduated in 1818.

These ten years in Italy were formative years for the poet. He spent most of his time travelling from Pavia to Cremona and Milan, mixing in the most prominent literary circles of the time. He had already decided that his interests lay in poetry, to which he would dedicate his life. Italy was, like Greece, another occupied country, whose young poets joined those romantic movements which had a political and patriotic character, with a strong neo-classical streak. At the university Solomos attended the classes of the well-known classicists, Giardini and Butturini. His interest in Greek Tragedy and Dante was shared by the other members of the Milan literary circles, the most prominent of whom was the poet Monti.

In 1818 Solomos returned to his native Zante. His friends were now young men who had also studied abroad and were interested in poetry. At their literary evenings, they improvised, in Greek or in Italian, given rhymes in light verse. They also wrote satirical verses, but Solomos between 1818 and 1824 wrote a number of short lyrics in Greek and Italian.

In 1828, after a dispute about the estate with his brother, Demetrios, with whom he was later reconciled, Solomos decided to move to Corfu. He had always been a recluse, so his decision to move to Corfu may have been the result of his gradual detachment from his Zante friends.

In Corfu Solomos wrote his major poems (published in English by Shoestring Press). His works took on an increasingly Greek Orthodox character. His friends translated Schlegel, Schiller, Schelling, Hegel and other German idealists for him, all of whom he read avidly, along with writings by Greek Fathers of the Church. Solomos left us only fragments of his major works, which he kept revising to the end of his life. He died from a stroke in Corfu in 1857.

SOLOMOS THE POET

Peter Mackridge, one of the most discerning Solomos' scholars, is also one of the few to place Solomos' poetry in its true perspective:

> Solomos was a deeply religious poet, indeed a deeply Christian one, but the religious outlook expressed in his poetry seems to encompass a broader spiritual experience than Christianity alone can offer. Yet, while he was clearly inspired by certain Platonic ideas, he avoided the temptation (unlike many of his fellow-Greek poets) to embellish his poetry with references to ancient Greek mythology.

(1)

What Mackridge rightly refers to as 'a broader spiritual experience than Christianity alone can offer' is Greek Orthodox Christianity. Solomos and the novelist Alexandros Papadiamantis (1851-1911) are the two major writers whose works are steeped in Greek Orthodox practice and theology. (2) Solomos' earliest poetry was religious. In 1815, at the age of seventeen, after leaving high school in Cremona, he wrote *Ode per prima messa,* which was influenced by Manzoni's *Inni Sacri.* From then on, Solomos' writings, whether they express his struggle to conquer a poetic language, to find an adequate vehicle to give utterance to the voice of the Nation or his struggle for a form, a style, generally a poetics, to accommodate that voice, are all encompassed by his faith. Besides his being widely read in European literature, classical and modern, as well as in the German philosophers, we know that the Scriptures, the writings of the Fathers of the Church and the Byzantine hymns, were part of his staple reading matter.

Throughout his life, Solomos had to cross borders, because of his bilingualism and biculturalism. Being born into the noble class of the Ionian Islands meant that he spoke and wrote in both Italian and Greek. (The common people spoke only Greek). The educational hiatus in early 19th century Greece, the result of 400 years of Turkish occupation, was filled in the Ionian Islands by the Greek Orthodox Church and by the importation of Italian culture (for the nobility), and in mainland Greece by the Church alone. What the young noblemen of the Ionian Islands sought in Italy was formal education, which was not available in Greece. Solomos himself in the draft of his Italian *"La Navicella greca" (The Greek*

Boat") tells us that he went to Italy a barbarian, but he did not return one.

When Solomos returned from Italy, there was very little Greek literature to match the European literatures upon which a young poet could draw. This, however, does not mean that the poet's Greek was poor, as George Seferis asserts in a puzzling text in which he also includes the poet Andreas Kalvos (Solomos' contemporary and compatriot) and C.P. Cavafy: '… And Solomos (is) a limit where poetry is purified as it approaches the inexpressible. Our three great dead poets who did not know any Greek.' (3) What Solomos lacked was a linguistic means in which to write his poetry, which could become the poetry of the Nation, as the latter emerged victorious from the Revolution. He was a true child of the age, greatly influenced by the Italian romantic movement, by his model Dante, and by the Zeitgeist, which demanded that the new poetry (romantic) was to be written in the vernacular. Solomos did not reinvent the Greek language, but by choosing to write in the vernacular, he established the kind of language that pointed to the future. His models were the Greek folk songs, the Cretan literature of the Renaissance (influenced by its European counterpart, but written in the local vernacular), and the Orthodox Patristic writings and Hymns. He had to struggle against the pedantry of the times, which supported the use of a purist form of Greek, a mixture of ancient Greek and modified modern features of the language. This was a language from above, which was not spoken by the people. It was in this polemical vein that he wrote his *Dialogue* on the language, in defence of demotic Greek. Three quotations from the *Dialogue*, spoken by Solomos' persona, the Poet, show that to Solomos language is not an end in itself but an instrument to take him beyond and help him cross another border in order to express the inexpressible that Seferis referred to. The poet in the *Dialogue* passes from 'I have nothing in mind except liberty and language' to 'first, subdue yourself to the language of the people, and if you are adequate, conquer it', and finally to 'There are two flames, … one in the mind, the other in the heart …', which shows the poet standing on the borderline and going beyond 18th century rationalism. Writing about how the demotic language in the Greek folk songs should be used, in a letter to his friend George Terzetti (1/6/1833) he has this to say:'…one should not stop there, one should raise oneself vertically'. (4) Mackridge again, in another text (5) borrowing Bakhtin's categories, shows how Solomos passed from the heteroglossia/polyglossia of his class to the monoglossia of the vernacular, and then again to the heteroglossia/monoglossia of his last years, when he returned to writing poetry in Italian. He moved beyond the choice of the common tongue: any language will do as long as it is adequate to express the inexpressible. But according to Mackridge, monoglossia can only be achieved through heteroglossia, and, therefore, the poet ends up with another absolute; a monoglossia which strives to express divine truth. In crossing borders Solomos takes antitheses, antinomies, oppositions, and fuses them in a truly Greek Orthodox way, as the end of the journey is the Absolute: there is no antagonism between body and soul, or mind and heart ('two flames'). This is not a stance that Solomos assumed as he matured in years, nor is it the result of his study of German philosophy. Iakovos Polylas, Solomos' first editor (1859) and disciple, in his *Prolegomena* (his Introduction to the poems) describes an incident from those early years in Italy, when Solomos in his late teens rejected the opposition mind/heart. It is worth quoting Polylas in full:

> Once in Milan he met Monti and they got to know each other. The famous poet was annoyed by the critical boldness of Solomos, who, despite being his staunch admirer, never hesitated to speak his mind. 'One should never think so hard' Monti said to him exasperated, while Solomos was interpreting a quotation by Dante, 'one must feel, feel.' The young poet retorted at once, 'First, the mind must firmly conceive, and then the heart must warmly feel what the mind has conceived. (6)

In his poetics Solomos tried to transcend another opposition, that of classicism and romanticism. G. Veloudis (7) in his examination of Solomos' German sources has shown that the poet throughout his life was haunted by a 'third mode', which he never realised. In one of his Italian notes to himself (as was his wont) on the Second Draft of the long, heroic poem *The Free Besieged*, Solomos tries to define his new mode:

> Take a spiritual force and make it strikingly concrete
> And break it up into a specific number of characters,
> male and female to which there must be correspondences
> in their execution etc. Think hard so that this must be done

romantically, or classically, if possible, or in a genuine, mixed mode. Homer is the greatest example of the second, Shakespeare of the first, and of the third I don't know. (8)

G. Veloudis notes that this pursuit of the 'third mode' was characteristic of all the European romantics, and to support his view that Solomos inclines to romanticism, he quotes another note by the poet written on the fair copy of his earlier poem, *Ode on the Death of Lord Byron:*

> The great difficulty the writer has ...does not lie in his effort to show imagination and passion, but to subordinate those two things in time and with effort to the meaning of Art. (But whether this is the old or the new, it matters not, as long as it is the Art which reminds you of the Great Mother). (9)

The sentence in brackets was added to the note by the poet at a later time, contemporary to that of the composition of *The Free Besieged,* which, as we shall see, is important. This bracketed sentence needs glossing: by new and old Art, Solomos means romantic and classical respectively. But what is the Great Mother? In his effort to prove that Solomos is a predominantly romantic poet, Veloudis writes: 'Solomos' predilection seems already to incline towards romantic 'Art', since its derivation from the 'Great Mother', namely 'Nature', belonged, as we have seen, to the theoretic/aesthetic arsenal of European romanticism'. (10) Veloudis, therefore, identifies the 'Great Mother' with Nature, but Polylas denies him as, in the text of *The Free Besieged,* in one of his Greek 'fillers', which he inserts in the poet's Italian text, he expressly identifies the 'Great Mother' with 'Motherland' (Greece) and, in the Italian text, the poet himself characterises her as 'Donna-Dea' (human divine), which gives her a Greek Orthodox dimension. It is worth quoting the Greek/Italian original text first, because Peter Thompson, in his English translation, leaves out the crucial 'Donna-Dea', thus stripping the text off an additional Greek-Orthodox element. The Greek bracketed line is by Polylas, while the Italian is by Solomos:

(Είναι προσωποποιημένη η Πατρίδα, η Μεγάλη Μητέρα,)
 Donna-Dea, perche senti tutti I dolori, e questi
raffinandosi nella sua grand'anima respiri il Paradiso.

Which Peter Thompson renders as:

> The land is given a human form – the Great Mother
> Incarnate – so that it feels all the adversities,
> And purging them in its ample soul breathes Paradise.
> (11)

Solomos transcends the tripartite problem of the classical/romantic third mode, because he subordinates it to the poetic result which, to him, is identified with 'Motherland' and 'Faith'. 'Donna-Dea' corresponds to the two natures of Christ (human/divine) and thus Motherland is re-born in the faith in Christ. This dual nature of Motherland is central in Greek Orthodox patristic writings. Interpreting the quotation above, George Metallenos notes the connection between Solomos' note and a speech by St. Kosmas of Aetolia, whom he quotes:

> Its characterisation as human/divine constitutes a secret concurrence between Solomos and Kosmas of Aetolia in the dual nature of Motherland, which is a purely Romaic-Greek Orthodox belief. 'My Motherland, the specious and futile, is Aghios of Arta, in the province of Apokoros ... We, Christians, have no Motherland here. That's why God has set our brains in the upper part of our body, so that we constantly contemplate the kingdom of heaven, our true Motherland'. (12)

Only in this light does the quotation from *The Free Besieged* above make sense, as it identifies Motherland with Donna-Dea whose 'ample soul breathes Paradise'. Lines like these, according to G. Metallenos, are not the result of poetic lyricism, but 'the surfacing of the theological – purely patristic – depth of Solomos'. (13)

Quoting Schiller, G. Veloudis may be right in claiming that the European Romantics saw the 'third mode' as a dialectical fusion of the classical/romantic, not in the same work or individual, but within the framework of historical evolution and a new working class (14). He is, however, wrong when he asserts that Solomos failed to see the historical dimension and so tried to impose an individual (therefore unhistorical) solution on a trans-individual (therefore historical) problem. Solomos, as we have seen, transcends the historical/unhistorical, ethical/unethical, classical/romantic oppositions, because his end is the a-historical Absolute, Seferis' inexpressible, as it manifests itself in history. Solomos has left us fragments and incomplete works, not because he wanted to keep up with the romantic fashion of the times (the 'unvollendetes werk' of German romanticism), but because he tried to achieve the herculean task of transcending history and language and show how human beings (ordinary people, heroes, freedom warriors) in a specific historical time and place through sacrifice and 'sin' can 'breathe Paradise'. This is both his greatness and his weakness. He left us a fragmentary corpus, because through language, poetry, and history he tried to transcend language, poetry, and history.

To close this general introduction to Solomos, I would like to quote more extensively from George Metallenos' book (15), which places the poet securely within the framework of the Greek Orthodox Church and shows with direct references to his poems (and this is only an infinitessimal sample) how conscious Solomos was of his faith:

> Against the 'Supreme Being' of the French Revolution he upholds the personal 'God of our Fathers', the 'Sublime' and 'Without Beginning Word'- Christ. (16) He is aware of the distinction between 'Created' and 'Uncreated', a fundamental characteristic of Orthodox Christianity. He refers to a god-Creator, who Himself is 'uncreated' and to 'creatures'. (17) This awareness differentiates him from any western naturalistic belief, because he does not allow for any dichotomy between the natural and the supernatural, since the eternal and the timely are interwined (Christ conveys his grace to man. (18)) The (created) world presupposes a Creator ... Nature is often personified but not deified. ... Within this framework we can view his references to the unearthly light from an orthodox angle. Freedom – his constant love – is bathed in light: 'Light in the hand, light in the foot, and all around you is light. (19) This is a truly Easter Sunday atmosphere 'Now all is bathed in light, the heaven and the earth and the nether world'. (20) This light is not physical-created because it pours out of the Holy Tabernacle, 'The Light of the Holy Tabernacle sweetly shimmers through the gate' (21) and it is heavenly ('the light that adorns you ... like sunshine and sparkles from

afar/ is not, not from the earth' (22). This unearthly nature of the light can be further substantiated by its correlation with the light of the Saints ('he can see the illumination flowing out before the Saints' (23) In this context I place his reference to the myrrh-smelling holy relics ('the relic that smells mellifluously') (24)

... Man in the Orthodox-thinking Solomos comes to his own in the Resurrection, in whose light he finds his true self. The resurrection, the highest feast in the Orthodox Church, which constitutes the eternal victory over death, holds a central position in Solomos' works.

Lambros is the most representative of these works.

LAMBROS

The Text: Iakovos Polylas, Solomos' desciple, was the first editor of the poet's works. In 1859, two years after the poet's death, Polylas published all the poems he had at his disposal (except for *The Woman of Zante*) to the great disappointment of Solomos' admirers and friends who expected a vaster corpus. As it turned out, only a handful of complete poems were published along with the longer works, which were incomplete or in fragments. This gave rise to an arcane mythology that somewhere there existed a treasure trove with the poet's complete works, but so far, with the exception of *The Woman of Zante,* no other work has come to light. All subsequent standard editions have more or less followed Polylas' choices, so the extant text of *Lambros* (in 37 sections) is what Polylas put together from what the poet left us, adding only a few explanatory prose passages. These are: a. the Plot in the beginning of the poem, which helps the reader follow the story, and b. shorter prose passages between the various sections, which in this edition are placed within brackets [ ], and act as explanatory notes and 'connectors'. All verses and the longer prose passages are by Solomos; the latter, originally in Italian, were translated into Greek by Polylas. However, even in this fragmentary form, *Lambros* can be easily read as a complete poem, with the prose passages acting as 'bridges' between the verses, thus leaving no gaps in the reader's grasp of the narrative. The verses are in the typically Italian metre, Dante's eleven-syllable ottava rima.

The poem's sections are grouped together into longer unities, which are given titles. Thus the whole poem has this form:

PLOT
MARIA'S GRUDGE (Sections 1-8)
MARIA'S DREAM (Section 9)
THE MARTYR (Section 10)
LAMBROS WITH HIS DAUGHTER (Sections 11-17)
TWO SONGS SUNG BY MARIA: 'The Two Siblings' (Section 18)
                         'The Mad Mother' (Section 19)
THE CONFESSION (Section 20)
EASTER SUNDAY (Sections 21-24)
MARIA'S PRAYER AND LAMBROS' VISION   (Section 25)
MARIA'S MADNESS (Section 26)
THE DEATH OF LAMBROS AND MARIA (Sections 27-31)
VARIOUS FRAGMENTS (Sections 32-37)

Chronology: Solomos revised *Lambros* over ten years, from 1824 to 1834. Polylas in his *Prolegomena* writes that three years after his return from Italy, Solomos was writing the song 'The Mad Mother' and probably 'The Two Siblings'. We know from a letter to his uncle, Stranis (dated 15/1/1822) that he completed 'The Mad Mother' in that year. Later he incorporated the two songs into the text of *Lambros*. He continued working on it in Corfu, where he moved permanently in 1828, and we know that he last revised the poem in 1833, and in particular, Section 25 (*Maria's Prayer and Lambros' Vision*), which he published in the periodical *Ionian Anthology (January 1834)*, the second poem he published in his lifetime. After that, he was absorbed in the composition of *The Free Besieged* and did not go back to *Lambros*. Polylas even quotes Solomos saying '*Lambros* will remain a fragment'.

The Poem: Polylas provides a summary of the story of *Lambros,* set a few years before the Greek Revolution. Lambros lives with Maria, a fifteen-year old young woman, with whom he has four children, one girl and three boys. However, he never marries her and commits the children to an orphanage. Fifteen years go by and, while fighting against Ali Pasha, he meets a young Turk, who turns out to be a fourteen-year old maiden who seeks refuge and asks to be christened by him. Lambros seduces her and then, to his horror, discovers the girl bears signs that prove her to be his lost daughter. In despair, the girl drowns herself in a lake. Lambros reveals the truth to Maria, who goes mad. It is Easter Sunday and Lambros is in church, where the ghosts of his three dead boys come to haunt him. He runs out of the church, takes to the hills and kills himself by throwing himself off a cliff into the lake. Maria, too, out of her mind, drowns herself seeking a better world.

Lambros' two themes are those of Motherland and Faith, as in virtually all of Solomos' works. In *Lambros,* the emphasis is more on Faith, as the struggle for national independence remains in the background, mainly to emphasise the freedom-fighting, noble, magnanimus aspect of Lambros' character, which is in striking contrast to his egotistical, arrogant, unrepenting side; the quintessential Romaic-Greek type. Solomos sees man 'outside any sense of binary realism (matter/spirit, body/soul). Man in Solomos has a oneness, natural and existential. The poet experiences and records, at the same time, both the grandeur and the tragic plight of ordinary man.' (25) Lambros is not modelled on the Byronic hero (as some critics (26) maintain and therein see the failure of the poem), not because he lacks Byronic characteristics, but, on the contrary, because in his Romaic-Greekness, he possesses them. In western societies, the Byronic hero was an out-of-the-ordinary outcast; while in the Greek 19th century society, he was the norm. In Lambros, Solomos describes the ordinary Greek type; he did not need to turn to Byron for a model. In the 19th century revolutionary Greece (and even in the 20th century) faith in Christ went hand in hand with the fight for freedom, and its 'practitioners' were ordinary, 'sinful' (Byronic, to western eyes), but, otherwise (to Greek eyes) unromantically heroic characters, like Lambros. Byron sets his hero against the hypocrisy of the middle classes, but Solomos had no social axe to grind, because revolutionary Greece was still, to a great extent, an organic society whose members shared the same faith and had a common goal: the struggle for freedom. Solomos prefers the term 'faith' to the more European 'religion', as the latter denotes a system with a set of beliefs, rules and regulations, which can be rationally substantiated, whereas faith is part of a way of life, which can never become the object of scientific research. Lambros eventually loses his faith; he does not transgress rules and regulations of a divine judiciary system presided over by an impersonal class-conscious God-castigator. To the English romantics, religion seems the pious luxury of a flaccid middle class' (27), and they, understandably make Prometheus one of their staple heroes (the Fallen Angel is another one). But to Solomos, Christ is a fellow traveller, not a Jupiter.

Nor is the romantic feature of the 'daemonic sublime' at work in *Lambros,* as Stephanos Rozanis asserts in comparing Shelley's *The Cenci* with Solomos' work, because, unlike Lambros, Shelley's character identifies himself with the fallen angel and very rightly so: 'The fall was the Substance. There was never any Holiness; or rather the Holiness was the fall per se.' (28) Yet neither Solomos, nor even Lambros, can be identified with the fallen angel, as a close reading of *Lambros* shows.

Lambros' name, very common in Greece, derives from the Greek word 'Λαμπρή' (Lambri), which means 'Easter' in the vernacular. The root word is the verb 'Λάμπω' (Lambo=shine), a verb connected with light, which plays a central role, literally and metaphorically, in the celebration of the Greek Easter and in Solomos' poetry. *Lambros* is set at Easter, which is the most important festival of the Orthodox Church, because the emphasis is on the Resurrection of Christ, since, without the fact of the Resurrection, faith is considered pointless. We cannot understand *Lambros* outside this theological framework.

This belief in the Resurrection is shown at the beginning of the poem *Maria's Grudge,* 2, where the last trumpet will rise the dead who are 'sleeping', a verb which in Greek, in its religious overtones, means 'die'. In Orthodox faith, the dead are 'sleepers' who will rise (the English word 'cemetery' derives from the Greek word 'κοιμητήριο', which means 'sleeping chamber'). The next section *Maria's Dream,* 9 has all the paraphernalia of romantic poetry (dream, ghosts, boat, Death, lake), with shades of Coleridge and Crabbe, to foreshadow the tragedy which follows. Section 10, *The Martyr,* is a prose passage which describes how Ali Pasha of Epirus, one of the most ruthless tyrants in pre-revolutionary Greece, tortures Maria's brother, a monk, and burns him alive. The monk, is a typical martyr, like the thousands who were tortured, burned to death, or impaled in Turkish occupied Greece and, who, like the free besieged of Missolonghi, attains sainthood. He is not the inflamed Bard of the romantics (Thomas Gray) or the daemonic visionary at the end of 'Kubla Khan'. Solomos places him securely within the tradition of the holy martyrs with his first reference to the Holy Light which is lit in churches in the midnight of the Resurrection before Easter Sunday: it glows but does not consume. Lambros, by name, should be the bearer of this light but he has lost his faith and dwells in darkness. The two songs, sung by Maria, 'The Two Siblings' and 'The Mad Mother' may seem out of place. With those two songs in four-syllable lines embedded in the text of

Lambros, Solomos imitates Byron, who, in *Don Juan* (Canto III) inserts the song 'The Isles of Greece'. However, the songs are organically connected with the themes of the poem. In 'The Two Siblings', the boy, Blossom, has lost his sister, Dawn, and looks for her everywhere. Finally, he finds her dead in the churchyard of the cemetery and believes she is sleeping. A wreath of white flowers has been put on her head, as is the custom for the unmarried dead. He picks up the wreath, takes it to his mother and comforts her by saying that if Dawn does not come back, she should put the wreath on his head. In 'The Mad Mother', two siblings are struck by lightning. Their mother goes mad, climbs the belfry, starts tolling the bells, and narrates how the children were buried.

The themes of these two songs are death, in the semblance of sleep (promise of resurrection), and madness, accompanied by the image of the wreath of flowers with which dead children are crowned. Maria herself craves for the wedding wreath, but instead she crowns her head with a wreath of wild herbs, before she, another mad mother, kills herself.

On Easter Sunday, Orthodox Christians celebrate Christ's Resurrection by holding candles of the holy light and by exchanging kisses accompanied by the happy announcement, which is also a greeting, 'Christ has Risen!'. This, for weeks afterwards, replaces all other forms of greeting when people meet. Section 21 ('Easter Sunday'), which describes this festive atmosphere in the church, repeats almost verbatim one of the hymns chanted in the Easter Sunday Mass:

> Day of Resurrection let us rejoice over the feast
> and embrace each other. Let us call brothers those who
> hate us; let us forgive everything on Resurrection Day,
> and let us cry out thus: Christ has risen from the dead,
> through death he stepped on death and gave life
> to those in the tombs.

The 'kiss of love' and the holy light are external symbols of the promised resurrection of the bodies in the Second Coming. Throughout *Lambros,* kisses exchanged are either bitter (associated with death) or sweet (associated with life). Thus, 'In the Two Siblings' the angel takes away Dawn's life with a sweet kiss (an innocent child); the Christians in church (Section 21) exchange sweet kisses, while nobody talks to Lambros or kisses him.

Instead, only his dead children, in his vision, kiss him and leave on his mouth the bitterness of the funerary cotton. This isolation from the community is his hell, which he acknowledges ('Hell? I believe there is!'):

> Resurrection, above all, means communication, interpersonal relationship. One walks towards one's Resurrection, because there is the Resurrected one and through him the Resurrected, those who live in the community of Christ. In a very Orthodox manner, the poet identifies isolation and seclusion with hell... An Orthodox text (Gerontiko) gives exactly the same interpretation for hell, in direct opposition to the relevant Dantesque mythology: '... and one does not see each other face to face, but each face is turned to the other's backside.' (Makarios the Egyptian, *Sayings*, P.G. 34, 257C-260A) (29)

Lambros dies alone, as there is nobody next to him to close his eyes, and 'not in the Lord's bosom' (Section 27), which emphasises his isolation, not only from human community, but from Christ (the Orthodox view of hell). All sins, no matter how heinous, are forgiven if one repents, and Lambros, after all did not commit such crimes. He refuses to marry Maria; he unwittingly sleeps with his daughter; and he is not responsible for the death of his children. It is his pride and egoism that bring him closer to his 'dark isolation, both physical and spiritual. He loses his faith and sees himself as a tragic hero, a victim of Fate, rather than a man endowed with free will ('oh, I've been struck by God's curse...', Section 20). *Lambros* could be seen as Solomos' Orthodox answer to the ineluctability of classical tragedy or the romantic exaltation of the rebel as a hero. Perhaps it constitutes his example of the conflation of the romantic and the classical, the 'genuine mixed mode' ('modo misto genuino') he had set his mind to. Theologically, Lambros, in his belief that some Higher Power harasses him or that he is damned, sounds like a Calvinist. This explains the 'blackness' that surrounds him, leads him to despair and causes him to commit his only serious crime; he kills himself on the very day that in churches people celebrate the triumph of life over death.

Maria also kills herself, but she has lost her mind and is extenuated. She craves a better world and she shows repentance: she confesses to being proud, and thus cleansed and in new robes, decides to meet her betters (Section 27). The whole episode shows Maria preparing herself spiritually to enter Christ's Kingdom symbolised as Christ's Festal Chamber where she needs to wear new clothes. In Orthodox practice this is equivalent to the Holy Eucharist, which is preceded by spiritual preparation and the mystery of the Holy Confession. Maria confesses her errors and now, cleansed, is ready for the communion with Christ. Once again, Solomos models his text on the Orthodox Mass (written by St. John Chrysostom in the 4th century), when, just before the priest invites the congregation to take the Holy Eucharist, he reads:

> Into the magnificence of thy Saints how shall I the unworthy enter? For should I also enter the Festal Chamber my robe betrays me. For it is not a festal garment and I shall be bound and cast out by the Angels. Cleanse my soul, oh Lord, from pollution and by thy Compassion save me.
> (The Holy Liturgy. Daytona Beach 1993)

Ironically, instead of the wedding wreath, Maria puts on her head a wreath of herbs (symbol of sainthood?) and hangs her daughter's braid of hair round her neck, like the albatross hanging from the mariner's neck (symbol of guilt and repentance).

In the beginning of this general introduction, I mentioned the spiritual relationship between Solomos (1798-1857) and the novelist, Alexandros Papadiamantis (1851-1911), also known as 'the saint of the Greek Letters'. They belonged to different generations but they are related because their works are firmly based on their faith in the Orthodox Church. Papadiamantis, who comes from the islands of Skiathos, wrote his novels and short stories in the turn of the century Athens in the now free Greek State. This was an Athens which was beginning to distance itself from the pre-revolutionary Orthodox roots, with a rising middle class imitating European manners: their pietism, Popish grandeur and a congregation increasingly adopting Protestant pietistic moralising and, inevitable hypocricy. The first signs of what has since become an established malaise in the Greek Orthodox Church were surfacing at that time: a clergy with a strong propensity to Popish grandeur and a congregation increasingly adopting Protestant pietistic/moralising features, both trends alien to the Orthodox

Patristic spirit. Papadiamantis' voice is raised in resistance to this situation. He was 'anti-European' as far as religious pietism and middle-class hypocrisy were concerned, while, at the same time, he translated European novelists and, for obvious reasons, he was greatly influenced by Dickens and Dostoyevski.

Papadiamantis deserves a more than desultory reference in this introduction, because on March 24, 1896, he published in the Athenian daily, *ACROPOLIS*, a short story entitled *Without a Wedding Wreath,* which in its outline and themes bears uncanny similarities to Solomos' *Lambros,* though very little happens in terms of action. The story, which is set in Athens at Easter, is this: Christina, a schoolmistress, lives with Panagis, a tavern owner, and despite Panagis' promises, they never marry. Because of this, she feels a social outcast and, ashamed and not wanting to expose herself, chooses to go to church only on the evening of Easter Sunday when mainly servants and governesses attend the service. Christina is a far cry from Maria as nowhere is the latter socially harassed or made to feel inferior. In Papadiamantis' Athens social classes are clearly demarcated, and pietistic hypocrisy has set in. Christina, another martyr, puts up with Panagis' infidelities. He has a number of illegitimate children, whom Christina takes home and brings up as if they are her own, though in truth she has none. The story ends with a confirmation that Christ will receive her into his kingdom.

However, there is a striking similarity between *Lambros* and *Without a Wedding Wreath,* which clearly shows their Orthodox origin. Papadiamantis describes an incident in the church:

> Two eight-month old babies in the arms of their young mothers, who were standing, rubbing shoulders, near a church pillar, on seeing each other, immediately acknoweledged each other and struck up a relationship; the one baby, pretty and kind and cheerful, reached out, a small soft hand towards the other, drew it close, and mumbled incomprehensible heavenly sounds. But the voice of the infant was loud and was clearly heard, and Giabis, the church warden, did not like noise. During the all-night services of Easter, he very often went round the clusters of women to take to task a poor working class mother, because her child cried. This man now hastened to reprimand that poor mother for the innocent mumblings of her infant.

Christina, standing nearby, thinks that the church warden has no right to interfere, as crying babies are allowed to receive the holy eucharist: 'How much longer will the severity of the officials be enforced and be taken out on the poor and the humble?' Quotations like these bring together Dickens and Papadiamantis, but they also show that the Solomos of *Lambros* survives in Papadiamantis. The innocent infants facing each other and making 'heavenly sounds' in church on Easter Sunday confirm the Orthodox faith in interpersonal communication. Hell is isolation and silence (physical and spiritual), the new-fangled values enforced by the Athenian middle class warden.

A NOTE ON THE TRANSLATION

The edition used for this translation is the standard edition : Λ. Πολίτης, *Διονυσίου Σολωμού, Άπαντα, Τόμος Πρώτος, ΠΟΙΗΜΑΤΑ, Ίκαρος Αθήνα 1971*. (L. Politis, Dionysios Solomos, Complete Works, vol. 1, POEMS, Ikaros, Athens 1971)

Solomos' and Polylas' use of grammatical tenses may sound unnatural in English, because they veer from the present tense to the past tense and vice versa. This makes for dramatic effect and partly for this reason and also to remain more faithful to the original I have retained some of their idiosyncratic grammar choices. In this edition, individual songs and poems are placed in inverted commas while the various sections of *Lambros* and titles of individual works are in italics.

NOTES
1. Dionysios Solomos, *The Free Besieged and Other Poems* (edited by Peter Mackridge), Shoestring Press, Nottingham, 2000, p.xxvi.
2. 'Brothers, wherever evil finds you,
   wherever your minds grow muddled,
   invoke Dionysios Solomos,
   invoke Alexandros Papadiamantis'
   Odysseus Elytis, *The Axion Esti*, Translated and annotated by E. Keeley and G. Savidis, Anvil Press.
3. Γ. Σεφέρης, 'Απορίες διαβάζοντας τον Κάλβο', ΔΟΚΙΜΕΣ, τόμος Α 1936-1947), Ίκαρος, σ. 63.
   (G. Seferis, 'Some queries on reading Kalvos', Essays, vol. 1, (1936-1947), Ikaros, p.63.)

4. Διονύσιος Σολωμός, Ποιήματα, τομ. 3 (Λ. Πολίτης), Ίκαρος, Αθήνα 1991, σ. 254.
(Dionysios Solomos, Poems, vol. 3, L. Politis, Ikaros, Athens 1991, p. 254.)
5. Peter Mackridge, *Ο Σολωμός μεταξύ πολυγλωσσίας και μονογλωσσίας, στον τόμο Ζητήματα Ιστορίας των Νεοελληνικών Γραμμάτων. Αφιέρωμα στον Κ. Θ. Δημαρά*, Θεσσαλονίκη, Παρατηρητής, 1994, σελ. 257-264.
(Peter Mackridge, 'Solomos between polyglossia and monoglossia', in *Issues Of the History of Greek Letters (A Tribute to K. Dimaras)* Thessaloniki 1999, pp. 257-264.)
6. Ιάκωβος Πολυλάς, '*Προλεγόμενα*', *Διονύσιος Σολωμός, 'Άπαντα, Τόμος Πρώτος, Ποιήματα*, Ίκαρος, Αθήνα 1971, σ. 12.
(Iakovos Polylas, 'Prolegomena' in Dionysios Solomos, *Complete Works*, vol. 1, *Poems*, Ikaros, Athens 1971, p.12.) Athens 1971, p.12)
7. Γιώργος Βελουδής, *Διονύσιος Σολωμός Ρωμαντική Ποίηση και Ποιητική. Οι Γερμανικές Πηγές*, Αθήνα, Γνώση, 1989.
(George Veloudis, *Dionysios Solomos, Romantic Poetry and Poetics. The German Sources*, Athens, Gnossi, 1989)
8. *Διονύσιος Σολωμός, Αυτόγραφα 'Έργα*, Επιμέλεια–Σημειώσεις Λ. Πολίτης, Τ.1, Φωτοτυπίες Τ.2. Τυπογραφικη Μεταγγραφή, Θεσσαλονίκη, Αριστοτέλειο Πανεπιστήμιο Θεσσαλονίκης 1964 (425Α 22-30).
(Dionysios Solomos, *Autograph Works*, edited and annotated by L. Politis, Aristotelian University of Thessaloniki, 1964 (425Α 22-30).)
9. Ibid., (196.28/198.10)
10. Veloudis, op.cit.
11. Dionysios Solomos, *The Free Besieged and Other Poems*, op.cit., pp.32-33.
12. Γ. Μεταλληνός, Ιχνηλασία Πνευματικής Σχοινοβασίας, Τέρτιος, Κατερίνη 1999, σ. 21. (G. Matallenos, *Tracing of Spiritual Tightroping*, Tertios, Katerini 1999, p.21.)
13. Ibid., p. 209.
14. Veloudis, op.cit.
15. Metallenos, op.cit., pp.211-213.
16. 'Ode per Prima Messa'.
17. 'The Poisoned Woman', stanzas 9 and 10.
    'Ode to the Death of Lord Byron', stanza 26.
    'To a Nun', stanza 1.
18. 'He props up the pillow/And comforts you.', 'To a Nun', (In my translation).
19. 'Hymn to Liberty', stanza 95.
20. 'Third Ode of the Resurrection Canon' by St. John of Damascus.
21. 'Ode to the death of Lord Byron', stanza 111

22. 'Hymn to Liberty', stanza 94.
23. Ibid. stanza 92.
24. 'The Death of the Orphan', l.13.
25. Metallenos, op.cit. p.213.
26. Ε. Κριαράς, *Διονύσιος, Σολωμός,* Εστία Αθήνα 1969. (σ. Kriaras, *Dionysios Solomos*, Estia, Athens 1969.)
27. J.R. Watson, *English Poetry of the Romantic Period* 1789-1830, Longman 1992, p.79.
28. Στέφανος Ροζάνης, *Σολωμικά,* Ίνδικτος, Αθήνα 2000, σ.19. (Stephanos Rozanis, Solomika, Indictos, Athens 2000, p.19)
29. Metallenos, op.cit., p.214.

LAMBROS
(FRAGMENTS)

PLOT

Lambros seduced Maria, a fifteen-year old maiden, by promising to marry her, and she bore him four children, a daughter and three boys, whom he committed to the orphanage. Fifteen years went by and Maria still lived in Lambros' house, unmarried, grieving over her sin, with a nagging thorn in her side; the fate of her children. Lambros appears indifferent and unfeeling to the sorrow of the unhappy mother. And in those days that vicious, but magnanimous, man joined the Greeks in their fight against Ali Pasha, spurred both by the just cause of the Greeks and by his wish to take revenge on the death of a Hieromonk, Maria's brother, whom the tyrant of Epirus had burnt alive. (At this point the poet had the opportunity – either by describing episodes or by other means unknown – to depict that holy man in his martyrdom, with holy visions prophesying the rebirth of Greece.) In Lambros' camp, and while he is working up the feelings of his fellow warriors with his eloquence, a young man, a Turk, turns up and warns them that on a certain day and place the Turks are going to attack them from ambush and destroy them. Then the young man seems to have something else to disclose to Lambros, whom he trusts, because Lambros rescued him from the wrath of the other warriors when he turned up in the camp. He reveals that he is actually a maiden who loathed her race, because she witnessed the sacrifice of a friend of hers, a Christian girl, and that she has come to love the Christians when she saw how peacefully that girl went to her death and because she remembers what that girl told her about the power of the Cross, she begs Lambros to christen her for the good that he did on that day. The beauty and the sensibility of the girl inspire strong love in Lambros and, soon enough, he manages to seduce the frail and sensitive girl, just as he had seduced many other girls with his persuasive manners and eloquence. Yet never before, and in no other woman's arms, did Lambros feel such sharp pangs of conscience; and, one day, charmed away by the fine gestures accompanying the girl's talk, he opens her right hand and reveals a cross of blood, and on her throat a plait; the tell-tale marks which Maria had made on her daughter when he was going to snatch her forever from her arms.

Lambros gives out a cry of horror, and the poor girl hears from her father's mouth about her terrible plight.

*

Lambros and his daughter are in a boat in the middle of a lake; the moon is up; she is sitting in the stern, away from her father, lest they touch each other. With her hair down over her face, keeping away from the light, and huddled up, she contemplates her plight. Lambros is rowing without looking at her. Suddenly, he hears a splash, he turns round – the daughter fell into the lake. Should he rescue her? or, better still, leave her? The latter thought prevails over his soul. He hastily leaves the lake in which his daughter's body is enveloped. On that very night, Easter Sunday Eve, Maria, who is in complete ignorance of all that has happened, stands alone at the window waiting for Lambros, and although Easter Sunday is dawning, she keeps singing sad songs. He arrives home and startles her because he looks terrified; cornered by the woman's questions, and dazed with fear, he confesses what befell him.

On the evening of Easter Sunday Maria is praying with a broken heart and with great humility. Lambros is in church, where he resorted in his despair, seeking solace; he eventually shows lack of faith in the power of repentance, and while he is trying to choke the voice of remorse, as he is wont to, and leave the church, Divine Justice sends him from the grave his three male children, who pursue him and obstruct his exit from the house of God, before kissing him on the mouth.

*

Maria, unable to bear up against such misfortunes, loses her mind and, poor soul, in her madness, among other things, demands to marry Lambros, who, in order to mollify her, makes specious preparations for the wedding.

*

Lambros in his despair jumps off a cliff and lands on the same spot where his daughter fell. Finally, Maria arrives at the place and, in her madness, she mistakes the deep of the lake, wherein she could see exactly the same sky, trees, and verdure for another world, and hoping to live there more peacefully, she gladly plunges into it and drowns herself.

MARIA'S GRUDGE

1
'He who can hear the dewdrop drip
Beholds my tribulations and laments.'

2
'D' you see those tombs? Some day therein
You, too, will lie asleep,
Until the last trumpet from above
Chooses to blow and rouse you from your sleep.'

3
'The only time I saw you shed a tear,
Was just before I was dishonoured in your bed.'

4
'I run to her and on her right hand
With a knife I scratch a cross of blood.'

5
'And if I hear a stranger's child
Saying 'Mother', it breaks my heart.'

6
'Hear it laughing, crying, and sleeping'.

7
'But always in my wretched bed,
Always death, misery, lament.'

8
'The day drags on wrapped in thought,
And following a grievous supper
Is a nightmare-ridden slumber.'

MARIA'S DREAM

9

(The dream Maria relates to Lambros foreshadows, according to a note by the Poet, the destruction in the poem; both she and her daughter were to die by drowning.)

It seems to me that in my dream,
I sail across an empty sea.
Alone, I fight wave and wind,
And you're not standing next to me.
My eyes can only see the sky,
Try as I might, in my perilous plight.
I gaze at it, help me, I say, without
Sail or rudder, I traverse the main.

And my three boys, upon these words
Jump boldly onto the boat,
Whose wooden boards, under the weight,
Begin to creak as if in dread;
Immanent Death emerges then,
And after they exchange the secret words,
In breathy voice and in a huddle,
With ragged oars they start to paddle.

With a wry smile on her lips
My daughter walks up to me,
In a shroud her body's wrapped,
All white and filled with wind;
But now, the hand she's raising
Before my eyes, has a pale gloss,
It's shaking like a reed,
And in the palm I see a cross.

Blood oozes from that cross
Black, black, as from a spring a-flowing;
My daughter then, with apprehensive look,
Feigns indisposed to succour me.

The more those oars beat the current,
The more it gathers force around me;
Lightning flashes full, tearing darkness asunder,
Followed by the resounding din of thunder.

The waves will toss us skywards,
We feel we're in the clouds,
And then, they'll plunge us downwards,
We fear that death abounds;
The oarsmen turn their faces
And curse me, 'Be damned', they say,
'The waves above us roll,
and the boat is foundering whole.'

While in that storm I stood
Before my gaping tomb,
And tossed and turned with sinewy limbs
But couldn't keep my head above the sea,
Now I lie upside down in bed,
Once warmed by sin,
And bitterly I cry, because I've never seen,
Hanging on my wall, the promised wedding wreath.

THE MARTYR

10

(As I have noted in the Plot the Draft of the poem included a priest who was sacrificed by Ali Pasha.)

They were burning the priest alive and Ali was shouting at his slaves,

Charcoal for the cur; spread it, spread it.

He had joy that passeth understanding. How? Is he resting on cool grass? And Ali is mocking at him. 'What is it, holy man? I can see that you are used to working miracles; you keep turning around without moving a hand or a foot, and you are all in one piece. Well done! Beg Jesus to save you as soon as possible.' Then the priest, parting his lips, which were parched by the glow of the charcoal, says: 'Blessed be this flame! I can hear flapping of wings coming from afar and bringing to me the scent of the lily. Oh, I can see you, holy Angel! Surely, you must have sprinkled this charcoal with dew, the same dew of the children in the furnace. What's he doing? He is extending the immortal finger and is writing in the air, as if on marble, with glowing lines, things beyond my comprehension.'

(The vision of the priest showed the death of the Patriarch and the Kings of the Holy Union, who were fighting against Freedom. He also saw heads of Turks rolling into the moat that surrounded besieged Missolonghi, and the inflamed Martyr shouted at them:)

Stay there; in the pit you won't be roused
By the cry of dogs or crows.

LAMBROS WITH HIS DAUGHTER

11
'He walked in haste and wasn't late;
Look at me to see his gaze.'

12
'Of sorrow's tussle, you've had your fill;
Come close, amorous filly.'

13
Alas, woman, with my own daughter!

14
And all around the ear can hear
Only the current, not the dripping oar.

15
The daughter sits in the stern quivering,
Her hair's down before her eyes,
Lest she sees the moon arise.

16
He reckons ...
That every obstacle his oar touches,
Is his daughter's body that he smashes.

17
And lest, when he's about to moor,
The wave thrusts her to the shore.

TWO SONGS
SUNG BY MARIA

(Maria is sitting at the window gazing at the sea and waiting for Lambros; the unappeased Mother sings, first, 'The Two Siblings' and, after a short pause, 'The Mad Mother'.)

The unhappy people (the poet notes) are wont to sing songs compatible with the state they are in.

18

THE TWO SIBLINGS SONG

Like constant stars,
The little angels,
Were sparkling forth
From the hands of the Creator.

And they cried: Hail,
Newly revealed Wonder!
And they got closer,
Entwining arms.

And, lo, how the buds
From the trees are falling,
The heat from the sun
Is overbearing.

They're falling upon
This land's lawn,
Just as wretched man's life
Is mown.

But where's Dawn?
Dusk's drawing near,
And pitch darkness,
Lies down on the ground.

He looks where there is
Tall cypress tree,
He looks at the spring;
But nowhere is she.

In the threshing ground, the vine,
The road he looks,
And finally cries:
'Dawn, my little Dawn!'

'My Dawn', was often
From his bosom drawn,
And another voice
Rejoined, 'My Dawn'.

Blossom thought
It must be little Dawn's
And hastily
Made for Dawn.

He looks for his mate,
Like a dove
In love,
But all's in vain.

He runs up and down,
Looks all around,
And cries out,
He never gives out.

In the distance the whiteness
Of a wall emerges
And, round it, blossom
The laurel and the myrtle.

But at the gate
A full-branched willow
Bloomless weeps
For man's fate.

He saw her standing
In the middle and cried out:
'My little Dawn, your blossom
Got such a fright.'

That said,
He goes up to her;
Little Dawn is silent,
Not a word.

A red pillow
He finds underneath,
A deathbed
Narrow and bitter.

A death wreath
Round the hair;
Her countenance
Is still fair.

Perhaps the Angel,
Who gets the message,
Has taken away her soul
With a sweet kiss.

Because a smile
Remains on her mouth,
You think she shouldn't
Be laid on the ground.

She's not dead
Look at her face;
She's sleeping, she's sleeping,
A deep sleep.

Gloom and terror
Of a restless dream
Bring pallor
To hand and lip.

He's been looking for her
And now he finds her.
He's standing still
Looking at her.

(He sits beside little Dawn)

An innocent butterfly
In the heat of the day
Flits and seeks
A refreshing breeze.

And then on a tomb
She happens to rest,
Where, suddenly,
A sweet breeze blows.

She can sense
The breath of the air,
But is too innocent to know
Where she's sitting, where.

'My soul,' cries out to her,
The mouth of the child;
The body does not know
That it has no life.

That it is in the place
Where there is no road
For the whitest light
Brightly to flow.

Sweet-sounding bell
Which summons from home
The old hermit
To say vespers.

Oh, bell, whenever
You' re summoning
To the myrrh-smelling feast,
Your echo is sweet.

But when, oh bell,
Innocent people die,
And you begin
A long-drawn-out lament – it's sore.

Don't stop the sound
You're making now;
But hold off, don't lament
A man's death yet.

And I will
Entreat nature
That no quake's tremor
Should ever lay you in ruins.

I catch sight
Of Hesperus' light
As it climbs high
In the empty embrace of the sky.

And, there, over
Little Dawn's deathbed,
The fresh breath
Of the evening whispers.

Scattering the blossoms
From the body of Dawn,
And lifting the hair
Of both Blossom and Dawn.

With slow hand
He removes the wreath,
He puts it on her head,
And then he takes it off.

'The day's drawing in;
Little Dawn, I must be off,
If I stay any longer,
I'm done in.

'Little Dawn, come along, if you don't,
You're forever disowned;
I dread, I dread,
The hour of the dead.

'Little Dawn, wake up,
Wake up, if they find you
Here alone,
You will die, too.'

He goes to his mother,
He finds her in tears,
And he says, 'Mother,
Don't cry, now, I'm here.'

'Little Dawn's sleeping,
It's true, it's true;
Mother, stop crying,
For I'm crying, too.

'Here's the wreath,
Don't close your eyes,
Or turn
Your head away.

'I leave it on your lap
And if little Dawn
Takes long to wake up,
You can crown me withal.'

19

THE MAD MOTHER
OR THE CEMETERY

SONG

Now that the starlit
Night has suddenly
Found us alone,
And there against the rocks
The sea is torn
Soundless.

Now that every heart
Is open
To sorrow, listen to
A story
That bites deep
Into the marrow.

In a cemetery
Two cypresses
Stand
Two siblings
Greening
Among the crosses.

When at midnight
The winds
Howl, if you could see
How they sway,
You'd have thought that they
Are crying out to the living.

Two poor siblings
Are sleeping underneath
The unawakening
Sleep of death,
And their mother
Has lost her mind.

Poor souls! They were playing
Where the tower
Stands, and the thunder
Struck, and left them
Lifeless,
Wretched souls.

With wreaths of roses,
Dressed in white,
They lowered them,
Embraced,
Into eternal
Oblivion.

No stray dog's bark
Could be heard;
Nor song
From mouth or bird
Or a twig-rustling breeze
Sweetly blowing.

A murmur of water
Spurting
And cooling
The tombstones
Faintly broke
The silence.

The only token
Of death left
Was the smell
Of incense
Pouring into
The emptiness.

(The wretched mother comes running thither.)

She stops, scents
The air,
And ponders –
Poor mother! –
As if trying
To remember something.

Close to the wall
She bends down and looks,
Sweetly grievous
She smiles
At the sepulchral
Bitter herbs.

To the clouds
To the stars
Delirious
She throws up her arms
And she cries and raves
Terribly.

Then she drops them
And she's in stupor,
And starts again
Groping
Her way
Around the wall.

She goes round and round
And finally into
The belfry
Which she mounts,
Careful to obliterate
All traces.

In the mute
Desolation
Was full-moon
Illumination,
Like the resplendent
Primeval Night.

But she, poor soul,
Out of her mind,
Looks all around
Terrified,
Seizes the bells,
Gives out a terrible cry.

'If only that horrible
Deep darkness
Would soon leave
The ravines;
Oh, how heavy
It lies upon my heart.

'It must go quickly,
I can't bear it.
It's like, it's like
The torn
Cloth that covered
The two children.'

Ding dong the church bells
Sound,
Ding dong in desolation
They resound
In reply
Horribly, horribly.

'From the desolate
Anafoneetra Monastery
The Solace
Of the desperate,
The two children
Had two amulets.

'In my bosom
They are kept,
With these amulets
I'll never lose sight
Of their tombs
Day and night.

Ding dong the church bells
Sound,
Ding dong in desolation
They resound
In reply
Horribly, horribly.

'Hoarse chanting,
Candles smoking,
The deathbed
Boards creaking;
Slow is the bell
And horrible.

'Yes, yes they're dead;
They lowered them
Into the dark –
I hear the thud –
They lowered them
Deeper, deeper.'

Ding dong the church bells
Sound,
Ding dong in desolation
They resound
In reply
Horribly, horribly.

'Why do you throw
Earth on them?
Don't, don't cover
The small bodies,
Which lie in sweet,
Sweet slumber.

'Tomorrow we'll pick
Some flowers,
Tomorrow we'll sing
Some songs,
On the multiflorous
First day of May.'

Ding dong the church bells
Sound,
Ding dong in desolation
They resound
In reply
Horribly, horribly.

Ding dong she struggled
With the clappers,
And started again,
Harping on the same,
Until her voice had
A deadly croak.

✶

And now a fresh
Breeze awakes
And whispers
Redolent of
The fragrance
Of the evening.

It even pierces
The leaves of the heart,
Like the spurts
Of fantasy,
Which paint
Happiness.

She, poor soul,
Inhales the air,
Deeply she felt it
Within her,
And, oh, she descends
Into despair.

✶

Sad-hearted,
She viewed
And counted
All the tombs
With a slow nod
Of the head.

✶

THE CONFESSION

20

(After Maria has ended her songs, Lambros returns from the lake where their daughter was drowned. Maria speaks to him:)

Lambro, I didn't expect you so early; I've been singing; but what's the matter?

> Your voice is hoarse, your eye's dim
> And your face looks blanched.

Lambros, without a word, flings a braid of hair at her, and she picks it up. 'Oh', she cries. What? Did you find your daughter dead in the wilderness? Or did you see this braid brushing against her neck as she was holding out her hand begging for bread? Did you see the cross in her palm?

> 'Oh, tell the truth, out with it.'

And Lambros:

> 'Catastrophe and grief! Such a terror
> That no man's soul can hold;
> Oh! I've been struck by God's curse
> In such a way!' And he breaks off;
> And then, slowly, in a frightened voice,
> 'Listen,' he says to her, 'poor woman,
> A horrible deed that I haven't told anyone;
> Shall I tell you?' And she says to him: 'Be quiet ...'

But Lambros discloses to her that he has, unwittingly, deflowered his own daughter. They both remain speechless. Finally, they flinch at the sound of the bells, because Easter Sunday is dawning; and then, they bring their lips close to exchange the kiss of Easter, but they don't.

EASTER SUNDAY

21

The dawn's breezy belated star
Presaged the brightest sun,
No cloud or mist
Cut across any sky niche;
And from there, the air
Softly blew so sweet in the face,
As if saying deep in the heart:
Life is sweet and death is black.

Christ has risen! Young, old and maidens,
Children, adults, all afoot;
In the laurel-bedecked churches
In the light of joy assemble;
Open peace-making arms
Before the Saints and exchange kisses;
Sweetly kiss, lip to lip,
Friends and foes, say Christ has Risen.

There are laurels on every tombstone,
And pretty babies in their mother's arms;
The psalm-singers chant
Mellifluously, eyes fixed on the icons;
Silver glitters, gold glitters
In the light of the tall candles;
Every face is lit up by the holy candle
Held in every Christian hand.

22

He goes out, because his vitals burn,
And the first man to see is the undertaker.

23

Nobody talks to him or gives
The sweet peace-making kiss.

24

He keeps knocking, as if hoping
To be heard in the bottom of Hell.

MARIA'S PRAYER
AND LAMBROS' VISION

THE EVENING OF EASTER SUNDAY

25

And Maria comes out into the fresh air
To cool the soreness within;
The night's sweet and no moon stares
To outshine the stars,
Multitudinous in all their perfection
They shine, alone or in clusters;
They, too, celebrate the Resurrection
On the glassy sea, which bears their reflection.

'I pull my hair to my lean dugs;
I cross my arms; Heavenly, divine!
Tell Him who today has risen
To take pity on poor Maria.
This is the day of Love. Hades has been defeated;
The vitals burn, the elements burn;
The blaze of the World rejoices
And towards Him its spark discharges.

'Heaven resounds with Hallelujahs;
Enamoured, it gravitates towards the Earth;
Even the drop of water, clinging
To the glass, is alive; Hallelujah to me and to it;
When the Gate crashed open,
What tumult was heard in the nether world!
The abyss rejoices and whitens;
The passing of the Saviour bullets.'

But Lambros remains in the church,
Where no human breath is heard.
He flits from one thought to the next;
His mind's a desolate, crumbling world.
He slowly comes out of the pew
A sigh welling up from his soul;
Only the strewn, fragrant laurels
In his path crackle underfoot.

He lowers his face like a sulphur-candle
And quietly he speaks these words:
'Deaf, motionless the Saints, like graves;
I cried out until late midnight.
Man (and let fate decree its own)
Is God of himself, and shows it
In abject misery; into my soul
Dive despair, and sleep.'

He makes for the door slowly and opens it.
A soft voice says to him, Christ has risen.
At the next door he jumps, and a small,
Similar voice tells him, Christ has risen.
At the third, he struggles to go,
And a third one tells him, Christ has risen.
Automatically the three doors
Open and close without a sound.

And now three, like brothers, desolate and strange,
Each one holding an extinguished candle,
Wherever he turns, wherever he goes,
Follow his desperate quick steps.
Dirty and large and all torn
Were the Easter clothes they wore.
Whether in the front or back pews,
The rustling rags follow suit.

They keep no distance at any one time in his run;
Here, there, up and down, to and fro.
Eight feet at once stamp on the floor,
They run ahead, and he can hear his own.
To evade, for a moment, the traces of Hades
He takes a long leap in vain,
Like the luminary which swiftly in summer
Spills over into a ten-fathom shooting star.

In such close proximity, they went thirty times
The round of the church, which booms and thunders.
It is drowned in incense
As if forty censers were there.
They keep running fast, and always

The living has those cobwebs in tow;
They bend down, confer secretly for long
And the cotton-wool moves, as if about to fall.

Oh, who saw Virgin Mary lift
Her hand to cover her eyes?
Oh! Who saw Christ at Easter
Sweating blood, and reddening all over?
What blight looms over the church,
Which, on that very day, resounded
With such revelling and chanting,
And was flooded with candlelight.

He's at the Holy Altar, he shivers
And falls on his knees before them.
In horror, he looks at them and cries out:
'I know you. What d' you want? You are mine.
The face of each one is like my own;
But speak, why do you crowd about me?
Forgive and give up – Go away;
It's too early for the Second Coming.

'Oh, you infernal creatures, unhand me.'
Then lips fasten on lips.
Each kiss given was a knife
Piercing the heart of that wretched man.
Not since primeval starlight
Were such kisses of terror given.
The lips spit out the poison;
The funerary cotton-wool was swallowed whole.

He stands there, motionless as marble, until dawn,
And the dead children are gone.
He raises his terrified head
And inhales heavy funerary incense.
At last he stares fiercely
At the laurels, and, after a while, cries:
'Off, with you, token of bliss' and with
Both fists, he strikes the Crucifix.

'Hell?' I believe there is; it's growing,
It's blazing in my vitals.
Tonight Somebody who does as he pleases
Has sent me my children from the grave.
Without me knowing her, yesterday,
Disgracefully he put my daughter in my arms.
The only thing left now is for him to destroy
Himself, because he has made me.'

He rises and makes for the plain.
He crosses fields and woods, mountains, ravines;
To his eyes all that's green is black,
The waters and the trees are black spots;
He ventures forth in great haste,
Without taking heed of the darkness he sees around him.
He still says he's haunted, he still
Hears death's cotton-wool in his mouth.

Thus, the murderer who has numerous crimes,
If sleep eventually closes his eyes,
And those secretly murdered together come forth,
All bloody, and stamp on his chest,
Leaps out of the warm bed naked,
'Help!' crying out vociferously,
And so abject is his mind that with open eyes
He sees them before him.

MARIA' S MADNESS

26

The priest is making the wedding preparations,
And the candles for the wedding are lit;
Lambros, terrified, cries out to her:
'Stand up, poor woman, come to me.'
On hearing Lambros' voice, she shudders,
And at once picks herself up
And sings, and, singing, she cries;
And he says to her, 'Don't cry, don't sing.'

THE DEATH OF LAMBROS
AND MARIA

27

And Lambros expired with his mouth wide open, not in the bosom of the Lord. But who will close his eyes? Where's Maria, poor Maria? She's left since early morning. She wandered alone on the plain, smiling, and the rays of the sun, which at sunrise invited all mortals to enjoy life, now rejoice in the calm waters of desolation; the centre of the lake was smooth and glassy, like a blue pupil of the eye, which remains undisturbed when no worry for the future affects it. But on the edge of the lake, here and there, the scattered trees around it, seem to the eye exactly as they in fact are. Poor Maria came to the place, after wandering in the vicinity, and seeing all objects reflected in there, in her disturbed mind, took this for another world; she hesitated, and, throwing up her long arms, with the smile of madness on her face, murmured: 'Surely, that must be a better world than this one, and I will prepare myself to go there. I'll see, shall I really see, if there, too, no merciful hand will be held out to me? Because, on this earth, for so long, I've been wandering full of pride among so many strange faces, as if I have just now appeared before them. I will go there; so I will put on my best clothes, lest the new, unknown faces down there, look down on me.'

That said, she lays her lean fingers on some wild herbs growing in that wilderness. She makes a wreath of them, sets it on her wretched head, and puts round her neck the much grievous braid of hair.

And into the wave, which she takes for a mirror,
Looks again, smiles, and takes the plunge.

28

And she sees in the clear waters
A different bright sky, different branches.

29

'I bend down here, and before me I unfurl
Inexplicable places of another world.'

30

While Maria is about to drown herself, she looks down and, seeing her shadow, says: 'So you want to follow me? So your life in this world has become a burden? Who are you? I don't remember seeing you before. And it is most strange that you follow me now that I am so unhappy; down there you look like a madwoman. Beware of men, of the scented flowers they hold to their chest, of their whispers, of their furtive looks ...'

31

(The poem was to close with the following simile, in which the fate of Lambros, his wife and children was depicted.)
There was a lean tree in a forest and it spread out its branches to another tree; four branches sproutimg from its trunk; a thunderbolt struck and left nothing behind but the earth on which they grew,

And not a twig was left,
For a lone-loving little bird to perch on,
In the dusk, or at dawn, to chirp on.

VARIOUS FRAGMENTS

32

Stepping on the sea crest
She stands without stirring the waters,
Which in their glassy depth
Did not reflect her godly stature.
With no breeze blowing, the moonlight
Shimmering near her
Flickered, as if desirous
To kiss her divine feet.

33

Whoever turns his eye there
To see the distant figure,
Gazes at the sea of Africa
Always foaming and always choppy.

34

You deadly willow with branches bending
Towards man's last abode.

35

If Zephyr doesn't touch its edge,
It sends a darkening immovable shadow.

36

He leans sweetly towards the harp.

37

And cries out: 'Oh Virgin Mary, Oh, Soul Saviour.'